Daniel T Phillips

The Political and Industrial Advantages of Arbitration

Daniel T Phillips

The Political and Industrial Advantages of Arbitration

ISBN/EAN: 9783337071783

Printed in Europe, USA, Canada, Australia, Japan

Cover: Foto ©Suzi / pixelio.de

More available books at **www.hansebooks.com**

The Political and Industrial Advantages

OF

Arbitration

BY

D. T. PHILLIPS (CHICAGO),

United States Consul, Cardiff.

PRICE—ONE SHILLING & SIXPENCE.

CARDIFF:
EVAN REES & CO., 30 & 32, BRIDGE STREET.
—
1899.

"When we were Boys together."

———

For the sake of "Auld Lang Syne."

THE AUTHOR

DEDICATES THIS LITTLE VOLUME TO HIS

HONOURED FRIEND,

ALFRED THOMAS, Esq., M.P.,

(Chairman of the Welsh Parliamentary Party),

WHOSE GENIAL DISPOSITION,

STERLING QUALITIES OF MIND AND HEART,

AND DEEP INTEREST IN QUESTIONS AFFECTING INDUSTRY,

COMMAND THE ESTEEM OF

HIS FELLOW-CITIZENS ALL OVER THE LAND.

CARDIFF.   FEBRUARY 11, 1899.

PART I.

Adjudication of Judge H. M. Edwards on the Essay—*The Political and Industrial Advantages of Arbitration.*

I RECEIVED six essays on this important subject. The *noms de plume* of the authors are respectively, *Homo, Q.C., Justice and Judgment, Pitt, M. Sylvester, and Homo.* All the competitors have adopted the same conception of the subject, confining the political advantages of arbitration to the beneficent results of international arbitration, and the industrial advantages to the results of the settlement of disputes between employers and employees. These essays, as one would naturally expect, vary in style and literary merit as well as in the thoroughness of treatment expected in a prize essay on such an absorbing question as arbitration. . . . . . . The first essential of a successful essay is a thorough and comprehensive treatment of the question under discussion. Literary polish and vigorous writing, although essential to the complete essay, are not a sufficient compensation for the want of exhaustive and philosophic investigation and research. I will now make a few comments on the essays before me.

1. *Homo* [i.] As there is another essay bearing the same nom de plume it is proper to state that the one now under consideration is written on twenty-four pages of legal cap paper, and begins thus : " Every reader of the current news and literature of the day," &c. This essay is well written, and contains many facts pertinent to the subject. A few sentences here and there are lacking in finish and compactness.

2. *Q.C.* A short essay of uniform strength in argument and expression, but necessarily incomplete in its treatment of the subject.

3. *Justice and Judgment.* Another essay similar in style and scope to that of " Q.C," and containing

but as light reference to the political advantages of arbitration.

4. *M. Sylvester.* Original in thought, epigrammatic in expression, and rich in suggestion—this is a correct criticism on this little essay. It bears the touch of a master hand.

5. *Pitt.* This is not by any means an elaborate essay, but it is exceedingly well-written, well-arranged, logical, and comprehensive.

" *Homo* (the Author's nom-de-plume). This is by far the most elaborate essay in the competition, and contains the most complete treatment of the subject. . . . . While the author treats the question of international arbitration at as great length as any of the other writers, he excels them all in his discussion of the industrial advantages of arbitration, and he is the only one who discusses the feasibility of compulsory arbitration. One of the essayists says that compulsory arbitration is a misnomer. Technically he may be

right ; but much has been done in this direction
already in other countries, and as it is one of the
grave problems which future legislation must solve,
no treatment of the subject is complete without a
reference to it."

"I award the first prize to *Homo*, the second
to *Pitt*, the third to *M. Sylvester.*"

The Political and Industrial Advantages of Arbitration.

SYNOPSIS:

INTRODUCTION.

DEFINITIONS (1) of *Arbitration*, (2) of *International* Arbitration, (3) of *Industrial* Arbitration.

PART I.

The Political Advantages of Arbitration :

1. It prevents the needless expenditure and waste of the people's money.

2. It strengthens the nation's character and safety.

3. It elevates the standard of public ethics throughout all nations.

4. It supplants misconceptions of national virility by loftier ideas.

5. It confirms the wisdom of the Monroe doctrine.

6. It promotes international comity.

PART II.

The Industrial Advantages of Arbitration :

1. It establishes the dignity of toil.

2. It saves employers and employees from financial losses.

3. It preserves society at large from incalculable injury.

4. It protects human life.

5. It adjusts wages amicably and equitably.

6. It tends toward the extermination of strikes.

7. It leads to favourable results all over the world.

8. It recognizes a third party, which is advantageous to all concerned.

9. It enlists the thoughtful interest of leading men, and leads to wholesome legislation.

10. It destines to usher in the halcyon era of industrial peace and undisturbed prosperity.

INTRODUCTION.

THE theme for our discussion is opportune. The writer assumes that the Committee had in mind the broadest view of the subject—Arbitration as it touches national and industrial life.

By *Arbitration*, we understand the hearing of disputes between two opposing factions before a committee selected for that purpose, whose decision upon the subject-matter in controversy shall be final. This decision is familiarly known as the " award."

In *International Arbitration*, leading represent-atives of different nations are chosen to hear and determine disputes between one government and another, as in the case of the " Alaska Fisheries " contention between the United States and Great Britain, and the " Territorial Boundary " controv-ersy between Venezuela and Great Britain.

In *Industrial Arbitration*, two or more men are chosen by Labour to champion its cause, and the same number are selected by Capital to advocate its claims. These appointees are at liberty to invite an outside party to act as chairman. He is supposed to be thoroughly unbiassed, impartial, independent, and competent. It is his prerogative to throw in his casting vote, should the votes of the contending parties be evenly divided—*i.e.*, if it be necessary to press the matter to a vote.

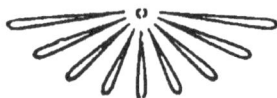

The Political and Industrial Advantages of Arbitration.

PART I.

I. *The Political Advantages of Arbitration.*

We presume that this political phase of the subject refers to Arbitration between one nation and another. What are the advantages of such an Arbitration ?

1. *It prevents the needless expenditure and waste of the people's money.*

No less than twenty nations are at the present time supporting a navy of 2,565 ships, and sixteen nations maintain upon a "peace-footing" a total force of 3,522,000 men.

It is doubtful whether the different governments in the past were more disposed to enjoy peace, even though they fought for it, or to persist in fighting, even though they had to keep peace periodically to recuperate for more war. At least it is far from certainty whether they were ready to abandon " the ethics of enmity and the policy of militancy for the ethics of amity and the policy of industrialism." The indications to-day seem favourable to pacific measures.

The needless waste and loss of maintaining relations between one nation and another by brute force are apparent to many, while it is held to be a necessary incident of national rivalry by a thinking few and an unthinking multitude. Of the destructiveness of militarism, it is hard to say anything new. The millions of precious lives lost, and the billions of valuable money spent, are fearful to contemplate. We turn away from the subject appalled and exasperated.

That there is a more excellent way has been frequently demonstrated within this present century. We recall the " Portendio " case between

France and England; in 1843 the "General Armstrong" case between the United States and Portugal, arbitrated by Louis Napoleon as President of the French Republic; the "Alabama" case, and the "Geneva Convention" of 1872 ; and the " Behring Straits " case, which, though not yet quite closed, will ere long be amicably settled.

Whether the attitude of President Cleveland in the Venezuelan controversy may have been for political effect or not, humane methods for the adjustment of international disputes have been the ultimate effect of the Venezuelan settlement. Lord Salisbury's spirit was most commendable during this delicate controversy.

2. *The strengthening of the nation's character and safety.*

Americans of the timid type have grown more and more suspicious of late that their national policy has become less peaceable and more poltroonish, gravitating so far into concern for

their material interests, that they have almost
forgotten their moral interests and obligations.
They are so easily excited. Of course no nation is
respectable that permits itself or its citizens to be
victimized. It is a part of the moral mission of
nations to be bulwarks of justice, at all hazards,
against every form of injustice. In so far as the
people of the United States have seemed to be
willing to tolerate wrong, rather than sacrifice the
money and the blood, if necessary, to right the
wrong, they have been culpable. It is easy however to criticize and find fault.

Nevertheless, while this phase of national obliga-
tion needs great consideration, there is more
immediate need of attention to other and restrain-
ing considerations. Nations defeat themselves and
obstruct their own development by pursuing
policies of violence in maintaining their dignity
against other nations. That nation is twice a
conqueror which restrains itself from wrong towards
another nation. The nation that subdues its own

impulse to triumph over another in an unjust cause, makes more gain for itself and for the world, than by forcibly conquering another nation, even in a righteous cause. It is not to be expected that the citizens will be free from the spirit of aggression in their domestic relations in a state which is aggressive in its foreign relations. Evident national purpose to deal equitably in all cases impressively endorses the principle that righteousness must be sovereign in normal nations as well as in individuals. Like all other moral actions, this right national conduct is thus demonstrably politic. It reacts upon individual character. On the other hand, private morality is undermined by immorality in national practice. "The nation that is in favour of arbitration is in the civilized attitude ; the nation that opposes arbitration is in the uncivilized attitude," thus writes Henry Norman in an article which appeared in the *London Chronicle*.

That nation is the strongest and safest which upholds the principle of Arbitration. Do we need an illustration of this fact? Behold the United States of America !

3. *The elevation of public ethics throughout the nations of the earth.*

When international arbitration shall be made the recognized tribunal for the adjustment of differences, it will lift the nations so co-operating, to the maintenance of rivalry, upon the level of their highest common conceptions of national ethics. Nations have it in their power to say that certain principles of action deserve respect, and that the nation which disregards these principles will be treated as an enemy of the rest. It is the duty of nations to take this position.

By the policy of Arbitration, powerful nations set an example which first crystallizes their own ideas of equity, and then elevates the standard of public ethics throughout the world. This was clearly illustrated in the " Alabama " case. By the treaty at Washington, which led to the Geneva Congress, three new rules of neutral conduct were recognized. The British Government expressly denied that these specific rules were a part of international law during the American Civil War. It was agreed, however, that these rules more distinctly defined principles of neutrality which had been recognized as parts of the international code. This was equivalent to a declaration that the more specific rules ought to be incorporated into international law. This more distinct definition of principles was thus equal to an addition to the moral law of nations. Two or more strong nations having accepted the addition, it soon came to be accepted by most other nations.

Despite needless intermeddling with the Transvaal government, heartless atrocities in Armenia, and centuries of oppression in Cuba, the entire civilized world to-day are pretty well united in the conviction, that sanguinary measures for the adjustment of difficulties or disputes have almost seen their last days. Arbitration is the civilizing agency that shall finally settle all international disturbances. No other means will be tolerated in the centuries to come. The standard of public ethics will be higher and healthier.

4. *The supplanting of misconceptions concerning national virility by loftier ideas.*

Considerable vigour has instinctively been felt, that war is necessary to cultivate national virility. A good deal of it still remains. It is feared by some that the quality of men will deteriorate if they do not sometimes resort to physical force. The corrective of this impression should be the perception that there are better ways to use bodily and mental and moral powers than in destroying men of less force. We may excel and become more excellent on the average without curtailing or limiting the freedom of others to do and be their best. Life on the plain of struggle for *excellence* taxes ampler powers and will develop nobler types than life on the plain of struggle for *existence*.

International expositions stimulate human energy more effectively than international campaigns. Machinery Hall, not the field of carnage, nor the sea-fight, sets the sturdiest tasks for the strongest men. This is especially felt to be true to-day, since both the arts of war and those of peace differ greatly in their demands upon their active agents from the like arts of earliest times. More finely organised bodies and minds are necessary for success in the peaceful art of modern life than less complex life demanded. On the other hand, most of 'the pride, pomp, and circumstances of glorious war' are gone forever. Often-times has it been said that ' Peace hath her victories no less renowned than war.' Soon the 'no less' will give way to 'more.' The next great war will be simply a long-distance-contest between money-lenders and machinery manufacturers. In such a war the real rivals will be out of sight and far away. Industry will be turned to the destruction of death-killing labour, and personal valor will be estimated by the amount of skill manifested in useful inventions. Brains not brawn, peaceful pursuits, not brutal battles will dominate in that day.

Of no nations may a higher standard of international conduct be plausibly demanded than of the United States. Uncle Sam claims to have achieved self-government on a more liberal scale than other nations have realised. The right of self-government is measured by capacity to govern self when passion is aroused. The sober second thought of that country should therefore be a determination not to flinch from national duty, but to discharge that duty by insisting that reason and not violence must be the arbiter when international differences arise.

War necessary to national virility indeed! Already is it conceded that war is barbarous, brutal, devilish. That being the verdict of public opinion, no self-respecting man can afford to stultify himself by attempting to maintain this old, threadbare, exploded theory.

The operations of Arbitration, in a large measure, are responsible for this happy change in public sentiment.

5. *The Confirmation of the Monroe doctrine.*

Assuredly this is one of the highest advantages. No man in whose breast patriotism burns can recall the message of 1823 without feeling the thrill which always moves men when they become conscious that the rights and liberties of humanity are given a broader scope.

The central idea of the Monroe doctrine is 'America for Americans.' The gateways of the Western Continent have been open to all nationalities. Concisely stated, the doctrine means (1), No more European Colonies on the American Continent, and those already established not to be interfered with ; (2), No extension of the European political system to any portion of the American hemisphere ; (3), No European interposition in the affairs of the Spanish-American Republics.

The Monroe doctrine never contemplated intervention by the United States Government in the internal affairs of the Latin-American States, neither did it contemplate a crusade against any vested European rights on that Continent. This is evident from the words of declaration. It was intended to serve as an authentic protest against any extension of European power and influence on that Continent, and in such a sense it has always touched the deepest patriotic public sentiment throughout the land.

This is the attitude of the doctrine in its bearing on the Venezuelan question, and for that reason the British Government expressed its willingness to have that matter settled by Arbitration. Secretary Seward in 1867, when the French attempted to aid the clerical and conservative party of Mexico to make Archduke Maximilian of Austria Emperor, so effectually applied the principle of Monroeism, that the attempt was crushed, and the would-be Emperor executed. Mr. Seward took the ground that the United States cannot and will not view the interposition of any force in this western hemisphere, by any European power for the purpose of oppression or control, in any light than as hostile to the interests of the American people. His active measures resulted in the French withdrawing from Mexican territory.

By a policy of delay and inaction the United States Government allowed foreign aggressions in Venezuela, until at last forbearance ceased to be a virtue. When our population did not aggregate over 20,000,000, President Polk declared that his government would not consent to the transfer of Yucatan either to Spain, Great Britain, or any other squabbling European power. With a population of over 70,000,000, we have been too indifferent to the cries of our helpless Sister Republics, and have allowed foreign powers too much license. Venezuela, nine times larger than England and Wales, two and a half times larger than Germany, with a population of 2,323,527, and yet the Government of British Guiana was in-structed to purchase guns and prepare to hold by force the territory in controversy.

Wise counsel since prevailed. A cable dis-patch from London was received in reply to a deputation from the International Arbitration League, stating that Lord Salisbury's desire was to extend Arbitration to those whose interests were affected, expressing the hope that England and the United States would give the world the first instance of the triumph of a principle which would tend more than anything to abolish war. Noble words! especially as the British Premier had been regarded as one of the chief stumbling-blocks in the way of Arbitration. All hail! Lord Salisbury.

6. *It promotes international comity.*

No one can over-estimate the advantage in this respect. Had Arbitration prevailed, the bitter strifes, which culminated in blood-red war would have been prevented, or checked. It is not only good for 'brethren to dwell together in unity,' but nations as well. Courtesy demands, not to say good breeding, that every effort be made to reach an amicable understanding between contending nations before they resort to sanguinary measures, which measures are brutalizing. Arbitration appears to be the remedy for the correction of international troubles. Its aim and spirit is to quench all animosities between nations, and foster international fellowship, and good will. There is no need of elaboration to urge this point. It speaks for itself.

SUPPLEMENTARY NOTES.

SINCE the awarding of this prize, the whole civilized world has been roused as never before for more civilized measures in the adjustment of international disputes. Mr. W. T. Stead deserves the special thanks of all nations for the heroism, heartiness and humanity, he has manifested in the international crusade for peace.

The genesis of this happy movement, it appears, must be traced back to the year 1894, when the Earl of Rosebery determined to approach the Russian Government to check the growth of armaments by an international agreement. Alexander III. was in accord with the suggestion, and 35,000 signatures in this country were appended to petitions in 1894 in favour of the project.

The rescript of the Czar, sent by Count Muravieff to all the foreign representatives stationed at St. Petersburg, is as follows :—

" The maintenance of general peace and a possible reduction of the excessive armaments which weigh upon all nations present themselves, in the existing condition of the whole world, as the ideal towards which the endeavours of all Governments should be directed.

" The humanitarian and magnanimous ideas of his Majesty the Emperor, my august master, have been won over to this view. In the conviction that this lofty aim is in conformity with the most essential interests and the legitimate views of all Powers, the Imperial Government thinks that the present moment would be very favourable to seeking, by means of international discussion, the most effectual means of ensuring to all peoples the benefits of a real and durable peace, and, above all, of putting an end to the progressive development of the present armaments.

" In the course of the last twenty years the longings for a general appeasement have grown especially pronounced in the consciences of civilised nations. The preservation of peace has been put forward as the object of international policy. It is in its name that great States have concluded between themselves powerful alliances ; it is the better to guarantee peace that they have developed in proportions hitherto unprecedented their military forces, and still continue to increase them, without shrinking from any sacrifice.

" All these efforts, nevertheless, have not yet

been able to bring about the beneficent results of the desired pacification. The financial charges following an upward march strike at the public prosperity at its very source.

" The intellectual and physical strength of the nations, labour and capital, are for the major part diverted from their natural application, and unproductively consumed. Hundreds of millions are devoted to acquiring terrible engines of destruction, which, though to-day regarded as the last word of science, are destined to-morrow to lose all value in consequence of some fresh discovery in the same field.

" National culture, economic progress, and the production of wealth are either paralysed or checked in their development. Moreover, in proportion as the armaments of each Power increase, so do they less and less fulfil the object which the Governments have set before themselves.

" The economic crises, due in great part to the

system of armaments *à outrance*, and the continual danger which lies in this massing of war material, are transforming the armed peace of our days into a crushing burden, which the peoples have more and more difficulty in bearing. It appears evident, then, that if this state of things were prolonged it would inevitably lead to the very cataclysm which it is desired to avert, and the horrors of which make every thinking man shudder in advance.

"To put an end to these incessant armaments and to seek the means of warding off the calamities which are threatening the whole world, such is the supreme duty which is to-day imposed on all States.

"Filled with this idea, his Majesty has been pleased to order me to propose to all the Governments whose representatives are accredited to the Imperial Court, the meeting of a Conference which would have to occupy itself with this grave problem.

"This Conference would be, by the help of God, a happy presage for the century which is about to

open. It would converge in one powerful focus
the efforts of all the States which are sincerely
seeking to make the great conception of universal
peace triumph over the elements of trouble and
discord.

"It would, at the same time, cement their
agreement by a corporate consecration of the
principles of equity and right, on which rest the
security of States and the welfare of peoples."

The Manifesto of the International Crusade of
Peace is as follows :—

" We appeal to our fellow-citizens, especially to
all those in positions of influence and authority, on
a subject of the gravest importance to our national
and social life.

" The Emperor of Russia, by inviting the
Government to a conference to arrest the growth
of armaments, gives the people an opportunity of
which it is their manifest duty to take prompt
advantage. In the words of John Morley, ' Never
was the moment more opportune.'

" By the resolute and zealous co-operation of public opinion, expressed with no uncertain sound through its recognized channels of the Press, the pulpit and the platform, and by the votes of representative bodies, the noble initiative of the Emperor will be crowned with success, and ithe Peace Conference will realize the fruitful results which it is designed to secure.

" We would, therefore, earnestly recommend that no time should be lost in making the response of the nations manifest, audible and universal, by every available constitutional means, especially by town and district meetings summoned by the mayors or chairmen, on requisition of the house-holders, for the purpose of passing resolutions :—
(1) In support of the bjects of the Rescript ;
(2) To strengthen her Majesty's Ministers in their expressed intention of giving energetic and hearty support to the proposals of the Emperor ; (3) To elect representatives to the national convention

charged with the arrangement of the international pilgrimage of peace.

"We, therefore, earnestly appeal to all our fellow-citizens, acting without party or sectarian bias, to co-operate as speedily as possible in the effort now being made to secure such a vigorous and comprehensive expression of the will of the people as will assure to her Majesty's Government the support of the nation in realising the earnest desire of the Tsar that 'something practical shall be done.'" ·

Hopeful symptoms! Surely the new century will develop a new and better era.

International arbitration is consonent with American ideas. The history of the United States demonstrates that the Government has been reluctant to resort to the arbitrament of arms.

American statesmen and public sentiment have always favoured international arbitration as the only rational policy to pursue between contending nations.. Hence their concurrence with the Czar's proposal for an international conference to discuss the arrest of armaments and the adoption of peaceful measures.

Max Nordan's famous epigrams deserve the attention of the United Kingdom and the United States :

."You are peaceful, may you be generous.
You are free, may you be wise.
You are superior, may you be hospitable.''

It is a cheering sign of the times, that the rescript of the Czar of Russia has met such a favourable reception. Not to speak of President McKinley, and other American leaders, the brain and heart of Europe are enlisted on the side of this humane proposal. The leading statesmen and citizens of dear old Britain give no uncertain sound on the question, and Her Gracious Majesty the Queen will heartily lend her aid. May the inspired prophecy soon be fulfilled when " nation shall not lift up sword against nation, and when they shall learn war no more."

PART II.

The Political and Industrial Advantages of Arbitration.

PART II.

The industrial advantages of Arbitration.

There is so much to be said on this phase of our subject, that we hardly know how to arrange our thoughts. What we may lack in logic, we trust that we shall make up in fidelity and thoroughness of treatment.

As an instance of the intense desire on the part of respectable organizations of Labour to discontinue the old method of settling industrial troubles, namely by strikes, the 'United Brotherhood of Carpenters and Joiners,' at its convention in Indianapolis, voted to transfer the sum of twenty thousand dollars from the Strike fund for the purpose of promoting education and organization.

At a Congress held at Chicago under the auspices of the City Civic Federation, where Capital and Labour were well represented, it was unanimously resolved : ' That this conference of Arbitration and Conciliation recommend, that a large national commission be established through the Civic Federation with the view to procure the wider application of the principles discussed at this Congress, and that we put ourselves on record as being in favour of conciliatory measures for the adjustment of industrial grievances.' The author was present when this motion passed.

The industrial advantages we classify as follows :

1. *It establishes the dignity of toil.*

Labour, hitherto, has been regarded as a degraded condition. The history of the past confirms this. It is positively revolting to read of its harsh treatment, and humiliating subjections in days past.

La Salle's cold irony contains too much realism. ' You believe, perhaps, fellow-labourers and citizens that you are human beings, that you are men. Speaking from the standpoint of political economy, you make a terrible mistake. You are nothing but a commodity, a high price for which, increases your numbers just the same as high price for stockings increase the number of stockings, if there are not enough of them—and you are swept away. Your number is diminished by smaller wages, by what Malthus calls the preventative and positive checks to population. Just as if you were vermin, against which society wages war.'

Goldsmith's lines appropriately fit in with this characterization.

" Ill fares the land, to hastening ills a prey,
Where wealth accumulates, and men decay ;
Princes and lords may flourish, or may fade.
A breath can make them, as a breath has made :
But a bold peasantry, their country's pride,
When once destroyed, can never be supplied."

Our sires were indeed treated as a commodity. Their condition was a life of serfdom. They were expected to rise at sun-dawn, and labour till sundown, take what wages were proffered them, and ask no questions. They were as helpless as slaves born in bondage. They were treated more like cattle than men. This condition continued down to the present generation. It was the exemplification of the ancient Welsh aphorism : ' Y trechaf treisied, a'r gwanaf gwaedded.' That night of servility and despotism is passing away. The era of a brighter day has already dawned. Working-men will no longer allow themselves to be treated as slaves, and submissively take what pittance may be offered them. They assert their manhood. They demand a fair wage for a fair day's labour. Industrial independence is to them a gem of costliest value. That independence they have determined to maintain. And while the industrial warfares of the past may have contributed to this independence and assertion of manhood, Arbitration has accomplished much more along this line.

Now that Arbitration is destined to supplant strikes in the settlement of industrial disputes, labour is no longer the objectionable thing it once appeared. The labouring man has no longer need to act the cringing sycophant, or fawn before any man. He can boldly march forward, with head erect, his face beaming upward to the light, for he belongs to the aristocracy of the Universe. The man who lives on the earnings of others, and does no work, be he monarch or millionaire, belongs to the pauper community ; the working man, be he ever so poor, if he respect himself, and earns his own livelihood, is a king among men.

Not until Arbitration asserted itself, did labour become the dignified object it now is. Arbitration recognizes that the labouring man has a grievance worthy to be considered, and thus labour is honoured.

2. *It saves employers and employees from financial losses.*

Owing to strikes, employers sometimes have been bankrupted, while in other instances, they

have sustained heavy losses : on account of a
large reserve fund, they have managed to save
themselves from utter financial ruin.

The greatest sufferer, however, is the dependent
workman. The termination of a strike finds him
involved in hopeless debt, which like a millstone
hangs on his neck as long as he lives. If he had a
home of his own, it has gone down in disaster,
either to satisfy the mortgagee, or the building
society ; if free from incumbrance, it has been sold,
or rather sacrificed to procure food for his family.
Thousands of homes, after years of struggle to
secure them, have thus been irretrievably lost.

The loss of wages, too, has been immense. The
total loss in the United States during the five
years prior to 1896, was sufficient to pay the
national debt. All this is money which might
have been saved, had Arbitration been allowed to
utter her voice. But what of the millions of
money that have been saved to both employer
and employee through the philanthropic medium

of Arbitration. If for no other reason than the financial advantages gained by this method, we would not hesitate to recommend *Compulsory Arbitration.*

3. *It preserves society at large from incalculable injury.*

Not only do the employer and the employee suffer on account of strikes, but private citizens and business people not immediately concerned in strikes, and that in many ways.

We observe how a serious labour dispute, such as occurred at Homestead, Pullman, Buffalo, Fall River, and lately in South Wales, arouses such a social as well as industrial antagonism as even to influence the power of political parties, the independence of thought and the peace of professional and commercial men, so as to make it difficult for either teacher or preacher, editor or statesman, jurist or sociologist to preserve that temperament which is a pre-requisite for a wise, social, and industrial solution, and a judicious adjustment of the controversy. Troops are called out, whether wisely or unwisely, to preserve the peace. It matters not whether this necessity be created by the actual strikers, or a gang of hoodlums, or hired agents of capital. The industrial peace of the country is disturbed, and infinite injury is done. The Homestead strike cost the state of Pennsylvania a round half million dollars. The Pullman strike, besides entailing untold personal losses to business and labouring men, involved a military expense of 244,457 dollars to the State of Illinois ; 205,963 dollars were for services in Chicago by the Militia.

The great coal-mine strike of May, 1893, in the United States, closed hundreds of factories, threw hundreds of thousands of men out of employment in those factories ; add to this the miners, mill-men, and others who were out of work, and they swell into the millions. This brought fearful destitution into many homes, and ruin into many lines of business.

President Andrews, formerly of Brown University, truthfully declares : 'Were it not for strikes, or the fear of strikes, conditions of labour would probably be somewhat worse than they are.'

Does it not seem lamentable, however, that men are constrained to do evil, that good may come ? We cannot advocate strikes as a measure of relief, any more than we can advocate them as a measure of civilization. When a strike occurs, it demoralizes society everywhere. When the members of the industrial family suffer, all the members of the Commonwealth likewise suffer.

When Arbitration is allowed to rule, all this injury to Society is prevented, and ' prevention,' we know, is better than cure.' The derailment of engines, the overturning of cars, the burning of freight, the demolition of houses and buildings belonging to ' outsiders,' is an unwise, yea, a vicious method of settling industrial differences. Hundreds of thousands of dollars' worth of valuable property, belonging to property-holders have been sacrificed to gratify the blood-thirsty revenge of an infuriated, incontrollable mob, many of whom were strikers, and others, thugs and loafers. These black sheep in the fold of labour, and the ferocious wolves outside the fold inflict untold injury upon the cause of labour, and upon Society in general.

Arbitration would obviate all this malicious mischief.

4. *It protects human life.*

How much Arbitration has already accomplished in this respect, eternity alone can tell.

How many innocent men, as well as guilty men, in the past have met revolting deaths, during the raging of a strike, it is impossible to tell, many of them worthy workmen, and others who were simply interested in the issue of the conflict. Besides the slaughter in cold blood of many innocent lives, who can compute the number of wives and children who have gradually starved to death, owing to the old brutal and bloody method of settling industrial disputes? How many under that same old regime have committed self-destruction? We need not furnish harrowing details.

Mr. Joseph D. Weeks in his pamphlet on 'labour differences' says: 'Of the utter folly of many Strikes, there can be no question. They have been doomed to defeat from the beginning. They have been undertaken in defiance of all economic laws, in ignorance of the real condition of trade, and without any just cause. They have wasted capital, and decreased the wealth of the country. They have brought hunger, misery, debt, have broken up homes, severed long associations, forced trade to other localities, and driven men, women and children into the very shadow of death.'

No rational man, therefore, can fail to protest against the wanton destruction of human life which a great strike is apt to provoke, nor can he fail to advocate the peaceful agency of Arbitration, which alone secures the concord and goodwill so much to be desired.

5. *It adjusts wages in an amicable and equitable manner.*

The trouble with wages in the past, has been that they have been so fluctuating, and hence so irritating to working men. Wages are not as stable and satisfactory as they might be, nor what they will be when Arbitration shall have full sway.

Only let us investigate the past history of the labour movement and we shall soon discover that Arbitration in America, at least, has contributed considerably towards the increase of wages. Our skilled workmen in the mill, the factory, the shop, are to-day earning twice what their sires did. A few years ago they earned three-fold more. The same might be said of coal miners. During their halcyon days, they too earned three-fold more than their fathers, and as the result many are living in comfort, if not in luxury, while thousands more might have enjoyed the same happy condition, but for their wastefulness and dissipation.

If there is a class of men who demand our special sympathy, and help, it is this class who toil amid such dangers and discomforts. If any class of men deserve substantial remuneration, it is this class of operatives, yet it is about the worst abused class in the land.

Notwithstanding all this, but for the intervention of Arbitration in times past, its condition would be infinitely more helpless than it is. It is only a question of time, and these brave men will receive better compensation for their arduous and perilous labours. Millmen, machinists, carpenters, bricklayers and other crafts are on a firmer and more satisfactory basis than their mining brethren. Hard as have been the times in the months and years past the millenium of skilled labour has already come. Strikes may have somewhat contributed toward this, but the chief agency has been Arbitration. When strikes failed in their designed purpose, Arbitration succeeded in its mission. The best wages paid to-day may be attributed chiefly to the efforts of Arbitration.

The following is the rate of wages paid to labour at the present time in the United States. We shall take two cities as samples of others.

CINCINNATI.

			Dollars.	
Bricklayers	...	...	4.00	per day.
Stone-cutters	...	...	3.25	,,
Carpenters	...	...	2.25	,,
Tailors ...	...	...	2.50	,,
Machinists	...	...	2.70	,,
Printers ...	...	...	2.50	(average)
Gas-fitters	...,	...	3.00	,,
Blacksmiths	...	...	3.00	,,
Iron Moulders	...	...	3.25	,,
Plumbers	...	...	2.75	,,
Tinners ...	...	...	2.50	,,
Bakers ...	...	...	2.00	,,

CHICAGO.

			Dollars.		
Bricklayers	...	...	4.00 pr-day (8 hrs)		
Stone-cutters	...	...	3.50	,,	,,
Carpenters	...	...	2.50	,,	,,
		(and	3.00)		

			Dollars.	
Tailors ...	...	...	3.00	pr-day (8 hrs)
Machinists	...	...	3.00	,, ,,
Printers	...	...	3.00	,, (average)
Gas-fitters	...	...	3.25	,, ,,
Blacksmiths	...	...	3.00	,, ,,
Iron Moulders ...	...	3.25	,, ,,
Plumbers	...	...	3.00	,, ,,
Tinners...	...	...	2.00	,, ,,
Bakers ...	...	...	2.25	,, ,,

Let this brief list suffice. It has been ascertained that Arbitration, (as well as good organization) has materially helped to bring about the desirable state of affairs.

6. *It tends toward the prevention of Strikes.*

It has already prevented many Strikes, and we can scarcely conceive of the untold happiness and prosperity which shall be ushered in upon us when Arbitration shall supplant the brutal method of settling industrial troubles by Strikes.

What are we to understand by the word 'Strike'? In one sense it is a disagreement between Capital and Labour. It is indeed an economic revolution, and can never be settled by theory or philosophy. It can be settled by the stern logic of events, or by peaceful Arbitration. The three factors of national government and private enterprize, namely, production, distribution and consumption constantly undergo some change in their relation to each other by reason of outside events, hence the need of adjustment to meet these varying conditions. In this re-arrangement comes all the difficulty. Capital, as a rule, has plenty of time to think, to calculate, and to plan, while labour has none. Labour learns the effect of every change only by direct application. This is one reason why labouring men feel averse to any innovation. They have been outwitted so often. The trouble is brought about in the attempt of Labour and Capital to accommodate themselves to new conditions, conditions attended by new ideas of theories. These changes may be made peacefully, or be followed by bloodshed. One thing is sure, the result of either always puts the human race one step in advance: 'Revolutions never go backward.'

A Strike never occurs unless one class of men feels convinced that another class is robbing them of the fruits of their labour. Their interests are not identical as they should be. They are diametrically opposed to each other. One strives for all the labour he can buy for a dollar, while the other contends for all the dollars he can buy for a given amount of labour. It is too much a question of dollars and cents, between both, with little honour, and no humanity. When Capital obtains the advantage it is termed 'business.' When Labour succeeds in making a point, it is called 'Strike.' All great thinkers recognise that labour has been greatly oppressed.

Carlyle says : 'It is not to die or even to die of hunger that makes a man wretched ; many men have died ; all men must die. But it is to live miserable, we know not why, to work, save, and gain nothing ; to be heart-worn, weary, yet isolated, unrelated, girt in with a cold universal *Laissez faire.*'

John Stuart Mills says : 'If the bulk of the human race are always to remain, as at present, slaves to toil in which they have no interest, for the bare necessities, and with all the intellectual and moral deficiencies which that implies . . . and with a sense of injustice ranking in their minds equally for what they have not, and what others have, I know not what there is which should make a person of any capacity of reason concern himself about the destinies of the human race.'

Herbert Spencer says : 'The citizens of a large nation, industrially organised, have reached their possible ideal of happiness when the producing, distributing and other activities are such that each citizen finds in them a place for all his energies and activities, and aptitudes, while he obtains the means of all his desires.'

Despite the pessimistic utterances of these great

thinkers and philosophers, we venture to affirm that there could have been no excuse for them, but for the unfortunate squabbles between Capital and Labour, and the determination of each to down the other, by means of lock-outs on the one hand, and of strikes on the other. Arbitration was an untried agency, comparatively speaking, in the days of these earlier celebrities. Spencer, who must have witnessed some of the good fruits of this measure, would have written in more hopeful terms to-day in view of what Arbitration has accomplished and is still accomplishing in the prevention of Strikes. In the approaching century Strikes will be voted out of existence.

7. *It recognizes a third party, which is advantageous to all concerned.*

There are three factors to-day in industrial economy, Labour, Capital, and the Public. Neither the first nor the second can ignore this third great factor, 'a forgotten man' as Judge Tuley, Chicago, so pertinently states it, 'whose interests and rights must more and more be considered.'

Arbitration now demands that the outside people must be taken into account in the adjustment of industrial grievances.

During the Buffalo and Homestead Strikes and the Riots of 1892, the late Ex-president Hayes observed 'That if the State was to be obliged, as seemed inevitable, to call out many thousands of troops at great expense on the occasion of an important industrial contest, it would also demand the right to take a hand a little earlier in the game.' No labourer, no employer, no unions of working-men, no combination of employers can declare any more that it is nobody else's business how they settle their differences. The growth of a new social conscience, the highest social and Christian ethics, demand, if the parties of the controversy cannot come to terms, that the public shall secure full official and sworn testimony as to all the facts germane to the dispute, and arbitrate between the contending parties."

Arbitration, that is worthy of the name recognizes this third party, and in every instance it has been beneficial industrially and socially.

8. *It leads to favourable results all over the world.*

We have such a mass of material on this subject, that we find condensation difficult. We shall begin at the furthest point from us.

(1). *Australia.*

The industrial experience of New South Wales in 1890, was not unlike that of Chicago in the summer of 1894. Sheep-raising is a leading industry in that distant land, and the Strike of the Shearers' Union in 1890, owing to the employment of *non-union* men led to Strikes of *union-men* engaged in the transportation of goods. They refused to handle the wool shorn by non-union labourers. The Strike grew, till at last the coal-miners were inolved, and almost every kind of productive pursuit was dragged into a controversy. Workmen on the one hand and employers on the other were strongly organized, and the struggle between them was paralyzing and disastrous.

The injury to the welfare of the Colony became so serious, that the Government appointed a commission to investigate Strikes and their remedies, analogous in its character to the Congress of Arbitration and Conciliation created by the Civic Federation four years ago in Chicago.

Arbitration was determined upon. The New South Wales commission consisted of eight workingmen, eight employers and a Chairman. The investigation was most exhaustive, and the outcome happy. The commission recognised at the start that not all controversies were capable of peaceable adjustment. The report states : 'No better method of dispersing the mists that surround a controversy like that under consideration, than a friendly conference. A very large experience has shown that the difficulty is often cleared up in this way and reduced to such dimensions as admit of fairly satisfactory settlement.' Having recommended private methods first for settling disputes, the Commission then suggests that the 'State maintain a permanent Board of Arbitration.' This board was first to conciliate, and 'stifle controversies in their incipiency.' This method failing, it was then its duty to arbitrate. The two crucial questions were: '*First,* should there be *compulsion* in bringing the controversy before the Board? *Second,* should there be *compulsion* as to the award?' After much deliberation it was unanimously resolved by the Commission to compel both in controversy to appear at the request of either one. The work of the Commission was a success, and Arbitration in New South Wales has been in high favour ever since.

(2). *France.*
Here they have ' Council of Experts,' which have

been very successful. In a recent enactment they
have provided for ' Conciliation and Arbitration in
collective disputes.' Official intervention in an
authoritative way is ruled out in this enactment.
The initiative belongs to the interested parties.
One or both of them may send a written appeal to
the local Justice of the Peace, who will immediately
notify the opposing parties. If three days elapse
without any answer, their silence is taken as a
refusal. When a favourable reply is received, the
Justice at once invites both parties to send delegates
to a Council appointed to hear both sides. If
Conciliation is reached the conditions are embodied
in a paper and signed by the members of the Conference. When mediation in this way has failed,
the Justice invites the parties to appoint one or
more Arbitrators, or to agree upon one common
Arbitrator. If this does not answer, each side may
have an equal number of Arbitrators, who are at
liberty to choose an umpire, if they cannot agree.
A report issued by the French ' Labour Bureau '

for the year 1895, shows the commercial and moral effectiveness of this kind of intervention. It has been successful from the first. In 1893, the first year of the enactment, no less than forty per cent. of labour difficulties were happily adjusted under the new law.

(3). *Belgium.*

This country largely adopts the French method of dealing with industrial disputes between employers and employees. During the first experience of this country along this line in 1891, twenty-seven Councils of experts were at work, and dealt with 5,078 cases, sixty-five per cent. of which were conciliated and arbitrated, while nearly the balance of the cases were arbitrated by private methods.

(4). *Switzerland.*

Twenty-five trades unions have Boards of Conciliation and Arbitration, and in some cantons they have been established by the cantonal governments. These have been uniformly successful in bringing about amicable and satisfactory arrangements between the working people and the employers.

(5). *Germany, Austria, Spain, Portugal, Sweden, and Denmark.*

Arbitration and Conciliation in these countries are generally managed by the courts, or the Civil Authorities.   In some of these countries wages are so depressing that there is little spirit in the people to demand advance or Arbitration.   When industrial disputes arise, Civil Arbitration promptly adjusts them.

(6). *Great Britain.*

Strange to say, *legislative* attempts to establish Arbitration in Great Britain have been failures. *Voluntary* attempts, however, have been marvellously successful. They may be broadly classified as trade-boards, joint commissions and district boards.   The principal features of each class are the same.

The Board of Conciliation and Arbitration connected with the North of England iron and steel industries has had an honourable and fruitful record. It was established in 1869, and is composed of one employer, and one operative from each miil, or establishment. The efficiency of this Board is amply attested. During the first twenty-two years of its existence, sixty wage versions were made, seven by mutual agreement ; thirty-three by sliding scales, and the remainder by Arbitration. The Standing Committee during the last thirty-six years have satisfactorily arranged over 1,200 cases by means of Arbitration and Conciliation. The moral effect of all this has been most noteworthy. Industrial concord and friendliness have supplanted industrial strife and distrust.

The same remark will apply to other sections of the British Empire. Many have been the advantages secured through the agency of Arbitration.

(7). *The United States.*

Hitherto Arbitration among us has been sought

usually after a long, bitter and exhaustive contest, when both Labour and Capital were thoroughly worn out, and the patience of the community completely spent. When Arbitration was finally decided upon by the contestants, and relief was realized, it was relief after ruin ; it was a calm, after a storm that wrecked business, homes, and lives.

It has been demonstrated in every city of that great commonwealth that Arbitration has succeeded where Strikes have failed. Unlike Strikes, which sometimes succeed, but bring untold misery on millions, Arbitration almost invariably succeeds and brings unspeakable blessings in its train. Scarcely a day passes but we read of the good offices of Arbitration in that Transatlantic country.

We have personally seen its good fruits in several States, whereby Strikes have been averted, thus saving thousands from being thrown out of employment, besides saving their families from untold sufferings

9. *It enlists the thoughtful interest of our leading citizens, and leads to healthful legislation.*

Never before was such an interest exhibited in
the cause of Labour by our foremost men as at present. Arbitration seems to be the watchword of the
hour. It is enthusiastically advocated by Jurists,
Clergymen, Merchants, Journalists, Statesmen and
others. It would require an octavo volume to
record what our great thinkers have said and
written on this subject.

Some years ago, Ex-Congressman Springer said :
' It is only through an awakened public sentiment,
that wholesome legislation can be secured,' and
suggested that the Industrial Congress then meeting at Willard Hall, Chicago, elect three men to
co-operate with the United States Congress, in
formulating measures for the settlement of industrial disputes.

For what it is worth, we shall introduce one of
Judge Tuley's utterances at that memorable Con-

gress. 'Force the workingmen to combine in
corporations, subject to legislative control, force
your capitalists to combine in corporations, and
then provide that they shall appoint their com-
mittees of Arbitration, and they shall meet in
January of each year, and shall settle these points
that give rise to Strikes. The penalty ought to be
a forfeiture of their rights as a corporation. Let it
be prompt and swift. You have got to have some
stringent measures, and you must have courts like
courts of Arbitration, that come directly from the
workingmen and from the capitalists.'

We make this quotation, not because of its
feasibility, or practicability, but to show the profound
interest taken by men of Tuley's calibre.

Four years ago, the whole country from Maine to
California, and from the lakes to the gulf was
moved with indignation at the cruel selfishness of
two or three corporations, who would not submit
theirdifferences with their employees to Arbitration.

With brazen effrontery they announced ' that there was nothing to arbitrate.' The entire people were stirred, and the outcome was the appointment of a National Strike Commission, consisting of Messrs. Wright, Kernan, and Worthington. It was an unbiassed tribunal. None criticized the decisions of this Commission, except the subsidized minions of the Press, who seemed bound hand and foot to Capital.

Without entering into detail, the report of the Commission pointed out the arrogant and unjust attitude of the Pullman Corporation toward their employees ; the illegal and dangerous methods of the General Railway Managers' Association ; the errors and weaknesses of the Labour organizations opposed to those great aggregations of Capital. It presented in a lucid manner the real causes which culminated in riot and carnage, and the mustering of the militia to crush the up-rising of the people.

The conditions prevailing at Pullman, Ill., is set forth at considerable length. The conclusion reached was: "That the conditions enabled the management at all times to insist with great vigor upon its assumed right to fix wages and rents absolutely, and repress that sort of independence which leads to labour organizations and their attempts at mediation, arbitration and, if need be, strikes." It is a well-known fact that the reductions of wages at Pullman, to off-set losses, threw the greater burden on Labour, so that the working-men in most instances hardly made enough to pay their rent to the Pullman Corporation, who owned the houses, and took advantage to deduct the rent out of those wages, so that the men had to depend on the charity of neighbours and the Country Poor Agent for something to eat. During those fearful and cruel cuts in wages, no reduction was made in the salaries of managers, superintendents, and other officers, who could have sustained a reduction much better than the men who worked in the shops. The report of the National Strike Commission states, that the refusal to cut down the high rents at Pullman was unfair and unwise, in view of the great and frequent reductions made in the tenants' wages. " Failure to make any concession, and the discharge of members of the committee who waited on the Pullman officials for some settlement, precipitated the strike."

Of the General Railway Managers' Association the same report states : " That like the Pullman Corporation, they refused to consider the question of arbitration. Had they done so, such a policy would have prevented the loss of life and sacrifice of property and wages occasioned by the strike." Referring to that great railway strike, which was a fatal mistake, the Commission questioned— " whether any legal authority, statutory or otherwise, can be found to justify some of the features of the General Managers' Association, which has all the effects of a pool, the extension of whose power would be dangerous to the people. . . . The refusal of the Association to recognize and deal with such a combination of labour as the

American Railway Union seems arrogant and absurd, when we consider its standing before the law, its assumptions, its past and obviously contemplated future action."

The report concludes with several recommendations—(1) " That a permanent United States Strike Commission be formed ": (the "Labor Commission Bill" will obviate the necessity of this). (2) "That the States establish systems of conciliation and arbitration similar to that in Massachusett,— and to render illegal, contracts requiring men not to join labour organizations, or to leave them as conditions of employment."

Nor is this all that Arbitration has done for the people. Several bills have been for years pending in Congress, which have contributed much toward solving the labour problem, namely, the bills of Messrs. Erdman, Springer, Tawney, and finally, the " Phillips Labor Commission Bill,' which was triumphantly passed June 1st, 1896. This bill provides for an industrial commission of twelve members—three representatives of Labour, three of Agriculture, three of Manufactures, three of Business—at a salary of 5000 dollars each member ; each group of members to have a legal adviser at a salary of 5000 dollars. The duties of the Commission are to investigate all questions pertaining to Labour, and kindred subjects, and to recommend legislation to Congress. This measure has received the earnest attention of capable men, fully competent to arrive at a wise and proper decision upon such questions. The times are ripe for such a measure—yea, fully ripe. In Carrol D. Wright's Third Annual Report, we find that from 1881 to 1886 there were 3,902 strikes in America. Establishments to the number of 21,304 were involved in those strikes, and 1,323,203 men thrown out of employment. The strikes for those six years entailed these losses :—

Loss to the Strikers   -   -   Dols. 51,814,723
    ,, Employers of Labour -   ,, 34,163,814
    ,, Workmen through Lock-outs ,, 8,157,717
Amount of aid contributed to Strikers ,, 4,430,595

Since the year 1886, still more distressing strikes have occurred ; some, as we have already observed, perfectly appalling. We have reason to hope that the end of such calamities is at hand. As the result of economic study, and wise labour legislation, we may expect to see the representatives of Capital and Labour seated around the same table, where the grievances and needs of all may be carefully and thoroughiy considered ; where the interests of all concerned may be dispassionately discussed, and satisfactorily settled.

10. *It destines to usher in the halcyon era of industrial peace, mutual fellowship, and undisturbed prosperity.*

Instead of pulling against each other, as they have so often done in the past, Capital and Labour will pull together ; instead of fighting each other like *fiends*, they will fight for one another like *friends*, and Peace, sweet Peace, like a bird of Paradise will hover with rapturous delight over the scene, and sing with supernatural sweetness its message of goodwill to all men. It is no Utopian dream. We predict that in the twentieth century Arbitration will supplant the barbarous method (which has too long prevailed) of settling industrial disputes by strikes and lock-outs.

When the brutish days of strikes and lock-outs are ended ; when the demoralizing strifes between Labour and Capital have ceased ; when fair-dealing and mutual goodwill shall universally reign, and the banner of peace and prosperity floats over the industrial world : it will be recognized that Arbitration was the foremost factor in the accomplishment of this jubilant culmination.

The Good Time Coming.

———

" THERE'S a good time coming, boys,
    A good time coming :
We may not live to see the day,
But earth shall glisten in the ray
    Of the good time coming.
Cannon balls may aid the truth,
    But thought's a weapon stronger ;
We'll win our battle by its aid ;
    Wait a little longer.

There's a good time coming, boys,
    A good time coming :
The pen shall supersede the sword ;
And right, not might, shall be the lord
    In the good time coming.
Worth, not birth, will rule mankind,
    And be acknowledged stronger,
The proper impulse has been given ;—
    Wait a little longer.

There's a good time coming, boys,
    A good time coming :

War in all men's eyes shall be
A monster of iniquity
   In the good time coming.
Nations shall not quarrel then,
   To prove which is the stronger ;
Nor slaughter men for glory's sake ;—
   Wait a little longer.

There's a good time coming, boys,
   A good time coming :
Hateful rivalries of creed
Shall not make their martyrs bleed
   In the good time coming.
Religion shall be shorn of pride,
   And flourish all the stronger ;
And charity shall trim her lamp ;
   Wait a little longer.

There's a good time coming, boys,
   A good time coming ;
And a poor man's family
Shall not be his misery
   In the good time coming.
Every child shall be a help
   To make his right arm stronger ;
The happier he the more he has ;—
   Wait a little longer.

There's a good time coming, boys,
   A good time coming :
Little children shall not toil
Under, or above, the soil
   In the good time coming ;
But shall play in healthful fields
   Till limbs and mind grow stronger ;
And every one shall read and write ;—
   Wait a little longer.

There's a good time coming, boys,
   A good time coming :
The people shall be temperate,
And shall love instead of hate,
   In the good time coming.
They shall use, and not abuse,
   And make all virtue stronger ;
The reformation has begun ;
   Wait a little longer.

There's a good time coming, boys,
   A good time coming :
Let us aid it all we can,
Every woman, every man,
   The good time coming.
Smallest helps, if rightly given,

Make the impulse stronger ;
'Twill be strong enough one day ;—
Wait a little longer."

APPENDIX.

SINCE the awarding of the prize to this treatise two years ago, the industrial world in certain localities has been terrifically shocked by contending forces, necessitating some changes in the relationship between Capital and Labour. These changes, however, do not affect the principles or position of this volume.

Various methods have been suggested for the adjustment of industrial grievances. One, the *laissez-faire*, or Competition method, assumes the existence and immutability of economic laws or forces, whose action is inevitable, and to which, untrammelled, must be committed the settlement of all industrial questions ; the other methods are— *conciliation, voluntary arbitration, strikes and lock-outs*, and *legislative enactments*. These latter four methods recognize within clearly defined limits the force of economic laws, but repudiate the contention that these laws are like those of the Medes and Persians—fixed and unalterable. They claim the right of interference under certain conditions. The *laissez faire* method is hardly worthy of an extended discussion in this day of grace ; the method of strikes and lockouts should be consigned to the limbo of the barbarous past. The only methods which deserve serious thought are those of Conciliation, Voluntary Arbitration, and Legislative Interference. Our preference is for the first ; when that fails, for the second ; and when both fail, we unhesitatingly announce ourselves in favour of the latter. At present, we confess that we know of no other remedy than Arbitration by law—And why not Arbitration by law ? Recent years echo, " Why not ? "

Objection to this principle has been advanced that such a compulsory scheme interferes with individual liberty ; that the question of wages is purely a " business arrangement " between the employer and employee. Without entering into an extended discussion upon this specious objection, we contend that neither master nor workman should covenant to dictate or accept terms that will not provide living wages. Arbitration is the court that decides what is fair and just between man and man ; the go-between to reconcile conflicting interests. It does not interfere with liberty, but with liberty falsely so-called. It would interfere with the tyranny and oppression of Capital on the one hand, and the rashness and recklessness of Labour on the other hand.

The late Prof. Jevons in discussing the theory of industrial legislation says : " The first step must be to rid our minds of the idea that there are any such things in social matters as abstract rights, absolute principles, indefeasible laws, unalterable rules, or anything whatever of an eternal and inflexible nature."

The *laissez faire* theory assumes what Prof. Jevons and this little book condemn. As Mr. Joseph

Weeks pertinently puts it : " This theory is most dangerous in its teachings and tendencies. The logical results of its application are strikes and lockouts. . . . If the theory of competition is sound, then these stoppages, these strikes, are not only justifiable but are absolutely necessary and commendable."

Arbitration is the antidote for the prevention of strikes and for their settlement. If it cannot be secured voluntarily, it must be secured legislatively, or compulsorily. By legal arbitration we understand, arbitration established by law and operated under a statute, with powers for enforcing amends or agreements. Such arbitration has been tried, and found to work satisfactorily. The most effective illustration of legal arbitration is seen in the *Conseils des Prud' hommes*, which for almost a century has existed in France and Belgium. These tribunals are established by law at the great industrial centres. They are invested with judicial power, but that authority is not used until an effort to reach an agreement has failed, then the side declining to accept conciliation is compelled to accept arbitration. The award made can be enforced the same as the decision of any other court of law. These *conseils* have been of incalculable benefit to French and Belgium industries.

In Great Britain and the United States, legal arbitration hitherto has not met with much favour. In 1824, all Acts as far as they pertained to the settling of labour disputes were consolidated and replaced by that of Act 5, George IV., Cap. 96 : "An Act to consolidate and amend the laws relative to the arbitration of disputes between master and workmen." This was patterned after the *Conseils des Prud' hommes* of ·France. It provided for the compulsory submission to arbitration, upon the request of either disputants, in certain trades and upon certain subjects. Rates of wages could only be established by mutual consent. The act is still in force, but appears quite inoperative. It is to be hoped that our law-makers may enact such legislation as shall forever put an end to strikes and lockouts. Such a measure has passed through the House of Representatives in Washington, calling for an Arbitration Board of twelve competent persons, representing the different trades and professions, and in all probability will pass both Houses of Congress, and be endorsed by President McKinley, whose brilliant statesmanship commands the admiration of all civilized nations.

At the risk of repetition, we emphasize our hope that the days of industrial warfare and mourning will soon be ended.

Capital and Labour should be friends, not foes ; they should fight for, not against each other. They should submit their difficulties to a competent and impartial tribunal for adjustment. Had wise counsel prevailed, the recent miners' agitations would not have plunged business and labour into the maelstrom of poverty and crime. Both employer (whether corporate or individual), and employee should trust each other as brethren. The workman should not labour simply for wages; that is a mere mercenary motive : he should serve from a principle of loyalty to the interests of his employer, and be whole-souled in his duties. The employer, on the other hand, should not squeeze from his workmen the largest amount of labour for the least possible remuneration ; that is inhuman. We unhesitatingly advocate the principle of co-operation.   It is the ideal position to take.   Both masters and men should proportionately share the profits and leakages of the industries with which they are identified.   This view might appear Quixotic to some minds, but to us it appears as feasible as it is equitable.

Many firms in Great Britain and the United States have adopted other commendable methods affecting their employees, which have proved mutually helpful and profitable. The latest example is that of the National Cash Register Company at Dayton, Ohio, Mr. J. H. Pat terson, President—truly an ideal industrial community.

The services of a high-salaried Superintendent is dispensed with ; his place is supplied by the "factory committee"; experienced mechanics, who have sole charge of the Manufacturing Department, and the employing of hands.

An Advance Club has been organized consisting of the heads of departments and their assistants, together with a number chosen from the rank and file of the operatives. They meet, at intervals, for the discussion of questions affecting their business ; also for receiving suggestions and complaints from the various departments.

The Company frequently provides entertainments by the use of Stereopticon pictures, for amusement and instruction. A school for salesmen has been started, where for six weeks prospective salesmen are trained for their vocation. Text-books are provided at the Company's expense.

Conventions are annually held for a whole week of all the salesmen to compare notes and make suggestions.

Semi-annually a series of prizes are offered, ranging from five to fifty dollars, for the best suggestions. These prizes aggregate 615 dollars, open to all, except heads of departments and assistants. During last year 4,000 suggestions were made, of which 1,100 were considered practicable. Moreover, connected with the factory buildings, which are in first-class sanitary condition, are a force of janitors in white uniform to keep the premises clean ; bath rooms for men and women are provided, who are entitled to weekly ablutions, occupying 20 minutes of the company's time. In the grounds, eight acres in extent, are flowers, shrubs, and vines. Twice a day a recess of 10 minutes is given for recreation ; in the winter the time is generally occupied with calisthenics. A large room on the fourth floor, formerly an attic, has been fitted for an attractive dining-room with all conveniences for luncheon. A piano is placed in the apartment. Luncheon consists of hot tea and coffee, a nourishing soup, hot vegetables or meat served at the expense of the Company. The young women pay a penny a day for special items. The cost of the luncheon—about two-and-a-half pence—is more than balanced by the increased output for their departments, which proves a good investment. Space does not permit us to particularize further than to add that the employees have library facilities, lectures by distinguished men, N.C.R. House of Usefulness, presided over by a deaconess, who devotes all her time to the moral and social welfare of the community ; N.C.R. Boys' Brigade, Penny Provident Bank, Mother's Guild, Young Women's Association, Industrial School, Cooking School, Choral Society, Young People's Society, Sunday School (500 average attendance), Advance Club Hall, Kindergarten Room, Women's Century Club, Men's Progress Club, Mechanics Club, Relief Association, &c., &c. No wonder the N.C.R. Company is a decided success.

Considerable interest has been aroused by the communications of Bishop Percival, Justice Edmund Fry and Sir E. J. Reed, on the industrial problem. Anglo-Saxons, who love free speech and a free Press, will be divided on this debate.

We vouchsafe no opinion on the merits of these interchanges of thought and expression. We claim the inherited, yea, the inherent privilege of expressing our "own individual view," a view forced upon us by recent disasters; that until the Golden Age dawn, which we have predicted, we shall need the arbitrament of law. Law? Yes, law—to control both employer and employee. As long as the master-and-slave feeling prevails, we need stringent legislation that shall insist on Arbitration. The dissident may exhaust his vocabulary and brand such a measure as Utopian, un-English, illogical, illiberal, inconsistent, imprac-ticable, irrational, and so forth; nevertheless, not until the spirit of the Carpenter of Nazareth be imbibed, and the golden rule observed, can we

hope to avoid distressing, distracting and destruct-
ive discords and strikes.

When love shall dominate and lead the employer
and employee into the Arcana of brotherhood,
there will be no further need of legislation, no
more demand for arbitration, for there will be
no more strikes to arbitrate, no more lockcuts to
harass Society.   In that industrial jubilee the
problem will be—What will become of our legal
luminaries and labour leaders ?   *Davus sum, non
Edipus.*   I cannot solve the question.

PRIZE TREATISES BY D. T. PHILLIPS.

SUBJECT.	PLACE.	ADJUDICATORS.
Paul's Epistle to Philemon	Maesteg.	Caledfryn
John the Baptist	Treorchy.	Huw Arwystl
Electricity and its future	Laleston.	Ap Caledfryn
Advantages of Ready Money	Cardiff.	Titus Lewis, F.R.S.
Religious Education	Llangynwyd.	Archdeacon Griffiths (Neath)
Best description of the Miser	Mountain Ash.	Dafydd Morganwg
Congregationalism in Swansea Valley	Swansea.	Dr. Thos. Rees (Swansea)
The Book of Job	Aberdare.	Rev. G. P. Evans ,,
Evolution and Human Responsibility	New York.	Dr. W. C. Roberts
Place and Influence of the working classes	,,	,,
Life and Character of Abraham Lincoln	,,	,,
Chinese Immigration	,,	Ap P. A. Mon
Technical Education	,,	Lewis Williams, Esq. (New York)
History of St. David's Benevolent Society	,,	Hon. Horatio Gates Jones
Protection versus Free Trade	Gomer, Ohio.	Hon. Ellis H. Roberts
Leading Events of the Eighteenth Century	Youngstown, Ohio.	Rev. Jenkin Lloyd Jones
Influence of current Philosophy on Christianity	Canal Dover, Ohio.	D. R. Williams, Esq.
Advantages and Disadvantages of Strikes	Chicago.	Thalamus
The Qualities of a Happy Home		Rev. Jenkin Lloyd Jones
Excellencies and Defects of the Daily Newspaper		Rev. John C. Jones
The Causes of Commercial Depression		,,
Rights of Women in Religious Services		,,
Moral condition of the world at the Advent of Christ	Shenandoah, Pa.	Rev. Bismark Davies.
English Story based on Welsh Scenery	Idaho Springs.	Dr. Fred Evans
The Tariff Question	Seattle.	E. C. Roberts, Esq.
The Welshman in America	Scranton, Pa.	Rev. W. A. Williams.
The Jewish Religion		Rev. Lot Lake.
Political Defects of the Welsh People	Denver.	Hon. H. M. Edwards.
Political and Industrial Advantages of Arbitration	,,	,,
The 19th Century in its Relation to the Past and Future	,,	,,

WORKS BY D. T. PHILLIPS,

UNITED STATES CONSUL, CARDIFF.

"The Heroes of Faith"

Cloth bound.   Price, One Dollar.   Third edition.

OPINIONS OF THE PRESS.

From The Independent—" These discourses are conceived strongly and delivered with an earnest seriousness which makes them effective. They have enough of that kind of thought which is implied in robust good sense, and plain talk. It is written with vigorous beauty, and makes its points well."

From The Examiner—" Marked by good exegesis, sound common sense, and a spiritual fervor that manifests itself in the numerous and pertinent practical lessons that are drawn from the lives of the various heroes."

PRESS OPINIONS *(continued)*.

From The Watchman—"These forceful and admirable discourses we cordially commend to our readers. They are a credit to the head and heart of the author. The Christian cannot fail to have his faith strengthened as he reads this wel-lwritten work."

From the National Baptist—"A volume of excellent sermons on the Eleventh Chapter of Hebrews. The sermons are well analyzed, well balanced, well discussed, and well applied."

From the New York Observer—"These discourses are full of the Gospel Spirit, of effective illustrations, direct statement and earnest appeal."

From the Religious Herald—This volume of twenty-two sermons, from one who has so often contributed to our columns we take pleasure in commending. It is not Mr. Phillips' first venture in authorship, and will not be his last, if he lives."

From the Baptist Weekly—"This volume is intended to exhibit the nature and efficacy of faith. They furnish chapters for instructive and entertaining reading."

The late Dr. W. W. Everts, in " Watchtower "— " The synopsis gives us an analysis of twenty-two chapters of a book of 223 pages. The discussion traverses scriptural annals, not over-looking general history in illustrating the potency of faith. The author's style is incisive and vigorous, and often attains rhetorical beauty. It is a comment composed for pastors and teachers, and will be a healthful book for the family and Sunday School library."

From the Lutheran Observer (Philadelphia)—" This is a sterling book, which we cheerfully commend to our readers."

From the Churchman (Baltimore)—" These are soul-stirring discourses, worthy of the genius of our genial citizen. The book deserves a wide circulation."

From the Baptist Standard (Chicago).—Mr. Phillips

keeps himself to his one aim—instruction and stimulus, not solution of puzzles, nor display of learning. The author leaves the record as it stands, and draws from it familiar lessons in which are the things new and old found there, always, by the "scribe instructed under the kingdom of heaven." The style of the book has the admirable quality of perfect clearness, the thought is always distinct in the author's own mind ; and the expression of the thought is in the English of that pure and strong vernacular which no mannerism of whatever sort can ever improve."

"The Life and Character of Abraham Lincoln."

Cloth bound. Twenty-five cents.

OPINIONS OF THE PRESS.

New York Herald—" A concise, readable little volume."

New York Times—" Pithy, pointed, and pleasing."

New York Sun—" An enjoyable, well written brochure."

Port Chester Journal—" We congratulate our genial fellow-citizen on the appearance of this delightfully written volume. It is well worthy of the price asked. Our readers will remember that Mr. Phillips won the prize for the best portraiture of the Martyr-President. He also at that time captured the other prize essays at the New York Eisteddfod, four in number."

Rev. W. C. Roberts, D.D.., President of Danville College, Ky., in his Adjudication made these observations—" The Adjudicator of the essays begs leave to say that he has read carefully those submitted for his examination, and been gratified beyond measure at finding them all full of well-digested thought, logically or psychologically arranged, and expressed in terse, correct and idiomatic English. There is scarcely a single error of Grammar, Syntax, or spelling in the seven essays. If the writers of any of them be born Welshmen, able to speak their mother tongue, they have performed a feat worthy of the highest commendation. Whilst may foreigners have learned the language well enough to speak or write it grammatically, very few have ever mastered it as to be able to write a long composition idiomaticaily correct. This is a very difficult task to perform.

In the essays on "Abraham Lincoln," the spelling, punctuation and grammar of every one shows careful training and much painstaking. They are admirable productions. The correctness and flexibility of the language leads me to think that the English and not the Welsh is the native language of the competitors. . . . The essay of "Loyalty" (the author's pseudonym) whilst it gives as many of the best and most important incidents of Mr. Lincoln's life as others have done, yet it groups them around six or seven leading traits of character. The incidents in every case set forth the traits under which they are cited. Those traits again when taken together make up a complete whole. After one has carefully read the essay, he sees before him a grand illustration in the life of Lincoln of urbanity, humor, carefulness, simplicity, honesty, and devotion to the cause of humanity. The whole is brought out in its harmony and completeness, as a noble character in a public man. I recommend that "Loyalty" receive the prize for the best essay on "Abraham Lincoln.""

Hon. T. L. James, Pres. Lincoln National Bank, New York—"I rejoice to learn that you have concluded to publish your essay on "Abraham Lincoln." As the Chairman of the Eisteddfod in which you distinguished yourself, I heard with profound interest the complimentary remarks of the Adjudicator on your production."

Hon. Robert T. Lincoln—"Many thanks for the

happy and able manner in which you have delineated my beloved father. I have read with interest bulkier books on his life, but have never enjoyed any work better than yours. You have a felicitous, original way of putting things."

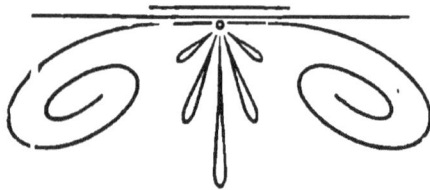

www.ingramcontent.com/pod-product-compliance
Lightning Source LLC
Chambersburg PA
CBHW031442280326
41927CB00038B/1570